Parenting
Business- Minded
Children

Quaneck R. Walkes

Dr. Quaneck R. Walkes

Copyright

Printed in the United States of America

First Printing, 2018

ISBN-13: 978-1721235957

ISBN-10: 1721235957

T AND P FAITH PUBLISHING

T and P Faith Publishing
1200 Broad Street #187
Sumter, SC 29150
www.tandpfaith.com

DEDICATION

This book is dedicated to my son, my superhero Daniel Walkes. And my Mother Emma Lee Richardson, the first small business woman that I knew.   Thank you both for all that you taught me.

Dr. Quaneck R. Walkes

Contents

Dr. Quaneck R. Walkes

ACKNOWLEDGMENTS

Thank you to my wonderful Uncle Toni who always encourage me "to never despise the very small beginnings because at least I have to chance to start over if needed." Thank you for many things over the years.

To my late Granddaddy Leroy Wells, Sr. Thank you for gifting me with the love of music and words. I never forgot when you said in 1997 at your kitchen table, " If she said is going to do something she will get it done regardless of how long it takes- it will get done." Thank you also for teaching me about loving people for who they are and not what they have, for having tools around and about!

To my Grandmothers Rosa Lee Wells and the late M. Elizabeth Richardson you both inspired me beyond what I can say in words!

Thank you to my late Uncle Levi Wells, who would listen to my nonsense both as a child and as an adult. Uncle Levi would tell me one day it will make sense. You encouraged me to be the best even if I had to sweep the floor. In fact my favorite job I had in church was cleaning. You encouraged me to "be the best floor sweeper and do the work that you were meant to do no matter how meager it may be to someone else."

To Joan Bell, THANK YOU!

The Difference Between and Entrepreneur and Business Person

As quietly as it is kept; there is a huge difference between a business- minded person and entrepreneur. For instance, if you are looking for someone who can keep a bottom line with an existing structure you should choose an business person. However if you are looking for someone who can get a bottom line in the black while being innovative than you should seek and entrepreneur.

For the purpose of this book we will concentrate on the business minded child and how to successfully parent them.

The Similarity of a Business- Minded Person vs. an Entrepreneur

Both types of individuals must understand the importance of networking, reading financial statements and establishing and keeping good moral within a company and industry. Both types of people have a level of responsibility that most people won't carry in that they must look at the overall success and or benefit of the company, clients and employees. In other words, they are tasked with responsibility of look at and making decisions from the whole picture instead of the slices of a pie.

Now that we have set the record straight; we will continue with our parenting series on examining how to successfully mold the business- minded child.

My Mother, Emma Lee The First Business Woman I Knew

The one thing that my mother taught me is to always write down my thoughts. She was notorious for writing down any issues that she saw. I never connected the dots until recently publishing another book, *Parenting business- minded children.*

As a child in elementary school, my mother was the first small business woman that I saw. She was a stay at home mother with a cosmologist degree. Nowadays, you may refer to a person who did hair in their kitchen as a kitchen beautician.

Most think that person does not have a license but contrary to popular belief, my mother not only had her license doing hair in our family kitchen but would take continuing education classes on Sundays. The continuing education classes also help me to obtain a great blessing 30 years later. When I was a child of Ms. Emma Lee, I often saw women come in and out of the house while my dad was at work and they would bring their children to play with us. Sometimes that was a good thing but sometimes it wasn't as when children are quiet that is when dirt is being done.

Moving on throughout life, I often looked back at how my mother would manage the house yet bring in income while never leaving it. Not sure if it was agreed upon between my dad and my mom; but one thing that I knew is that she did not let being a mother and a housewife deter her from making her own money.

Honestly, I think that is why I was able to become an entrepreneur during my first marriage and during the tedious divorce while being a single mother. It was because I first saw it at home at a very young age.

Sir Thomas Browne in *Religio Medici* (1642) concluded when citing 1 Timothy 5, "Charity begins at home." Also proverbs 22; 6 "Train up a child the way they should go and they will never depart from it." After much consideration and experience, I realize how my mother Emma Lee shaped my business and entrepreneurial mindset.

This is evident as I never saw any drawbacks to having children or how being a wife would not stop the influx of money from being drawn to you. It is my belief that money making is actually a mindset and the sprit to carry on. Trust me it can hear its name and do what you say it can do.

Because of how my mother trained me, as an adult while single parenting, I was able to create several businesses. Little to be known to me, one of my children was taking notes although she wasn't around most of the time. My Lil lady organized a board of directors, changed the way she dressed and had a business name. I believed in her so much that she also has had a logo for over a year. When asked how she learned that she needed to seek the opinions of well knowledgeable persons she said she just did what I do.

Ask Goal – Oriented Questions

One of my other children, Daniel would experience this every school day when he was in middle school. I would ask him what his goal of the day is. Daniel often didn't like it. However when he was in many college preparatory seminars, they would ask, "What are your goals?

When he refused to give me an answer, I would tell him "Even two year old children have goals. Many of their goals involve outside and candy. But they are still goals never the less." "Four and five-year-olds have goals of attempting to get out of nap time yet that is still a goal." If you catch my drift that goals start at a very young age, It is often noticed when asking, "What do you want to do today?" or "Did you have fun today" and "Did what you wanted to do?" Regardless of how it is worded, it is still a goal.

When parenting business-minded children, it is helpful to not only let them tell you their goals but to allow them to write it down. *Habakkuk 2:2-3* in the Bible states, "to write the vision so that an angel can run with it for it is set for an appointed time." Therefore, help your business-minded children write down their end goals. Then allow them to write three steps in which they will take to get it done.

If they do all of the steps on the first try great if not, encourage them to continue to work at it until they get it done or until they found out that is tht wrong step to take.

Remember the words of my mother Mrs. Emma Lee "Rome wasn't built in a day." My mother loved telling me that all my life and to this day, I am telling my kids, students and the clients that are getting parental mediation the very same thing!" And you know what I have found that statement to be true in everything that I have done and the things that I plan to do.

Reading is Essential

Thomas Curley, one of the best self-made millionaires known in the US and aboard Curley found out that "65% of those self-made millionaires were required by their parents to always read at least 3 books per month." Studying make the brain work faster and smarter. Just like the stomach is feed by food; the brain is fed with information. Parents who insists that their children read history, nonfiction, hobby books, business books usually quiz their children about what they had read. These methods of reading engagements helps to create the business- minded child.

No matter how busy your schedule might be, never leave your work of parenting your business- minded children to someone else such as nannies, grandparents, school teachers, and tutors. As parents, you must do your part. Remember, if you want a return on investment, you as the parent must introduce your children to Uncle R.O.I. investment. No investment of time and redirection when needed equals no returns when the children becomes an adult. Tyler Perry has proven this in his movie, Meet the Browns. Remember the dad who was too busy working while the mother had to struggle? Kids remember how you treat them. So when you put money over quality time with a business-minded child you will produce something incredible horrid.

Doing this is defiling your kids. It is never enough to spend just money on education, it is far better to spend time on educating them too. The stepping stone to academic excellence is made with early home promotion of literacy along with parents encouraging good study habits.

I remember being told that I could travel anywhere if I learn to read and write. The teacher who told me this was talking only of the imagination but I found it to be true as I have travel, currently traveling and have met persons from all over the world because I not only write well but I read well to.

In fact, one of my children Olivia has impeccable writing skills. This is contributed because as part of my discipline method; I encourage her to copy out of a book that is much advance. This helps to foster many things. It helps her to develop excellent penmanship, learn she is not only reading by writing but to start an inquiry of why and how. This method of discipline also helps her to learn something beyond what is being taught in school as a result she also is able to teach me too. Life-long learning is a multidimensional trait for producing healthy relationships.

From the experience of parenting business-minded children, I realize the world is made of billions of humans, yet few are billionaires. It is great to reach for that level but it is even better to appreciate where the business is before reaching plateaus. Billionaires who are only business minded have great ideas that have hone current up and running inventions and businesses. Business-minded children learned what others skipped are able to ride on the radar of success because of ideas they have furthered nurtured and developed.

Such is seen through mastery of vocabulary, letters, phonetics and writing skills later translated to multi-level academic successes. The joy of winning in this aspect of life gives business-minded children the courage to challenge future barriers to become more successful.

Talking is the Art of Networking

Many people would agree that when parenting the business-minded child, there are a lot of don'ts that you must allow the child to do. For instance, every child is taught to never talk to strangers however those with the business-minded personality know that communication and networking are essential when building a brand. So while you want your child to be safe; you must allow them to not be afraid of talking to people especially when someone says no.

Speaking of saying No, it is actually good for your child to experience rejection from either the parent or others. This helps with instilling discipline, self-confidence and to experience the unknown and helps when making a lot of mistakes, a parent must allow that child to experience the hard knock life. Sometimes even the parent must experience the power of the No when influencing the direction of business- minded children.

Believe it or not, the "No" and hard times helps the business-minded child understand things will happen, however as they do, it gives an opportunity to rethink and retry things. When getting rejected it helps to harness perseverance and stick-ability in spite of anything. When experiencing the unknown, this can be good for both the parent and the child as they must develop, explore and grow together. Business-minded children learns to express themselves more creatively than those who don't understand that even a good thing can be made great.

Lastly, mistakes are stepping stones to showing and evaluating growth. If one never fails, how would you evaluate success? You cannot unless you have made mistakes. Mistakes have a way of teaching you more than you want to know at times yet more of what you need to know every time.

When parenting business-minded children; you must let that

child do adult things like have goals and figure out how to achieve them. When allowing business-minded children the ability to jot down their ideas, parents must realize that business- minded children will seek ways beyond what is written on paper. Business-minded children will look at a person, product or services and think that their particular product or service will benefit that person, place or thing before a conversation is even started. They will take notes on how to make that sale to increase their bottom line.

HEALTHY Personal And Professional RELATIONSHIPS Is Essential For Growth

For psychological well-being, children's growth and success; it is imperative of parents to always connect business- minded children with peers of their own age as every child still deserves a childhood. My maternal family has taught me that while we work hard; we play harder. Children are playful and need playmates. Meaningful relationships is essential for both quality of life and any business venture. In fact, most successful business owners have some type of stress outlet or an enjoyable hobby.

Even office work requires friends who make you feel better and happy. Children with poor relationships perform poorly in school, get into trouble and develop psychiatric problems which can hinder them later in life as an adult. Parenting involves making your child foster healthy and strong relationships with play dates, friends and allow them to participate in activities they enjoy.

My childhood was full of hardship and meager accomplishments. For instance, I graduated from high school with a 1.9 GPA. That's right that is a D average. Remember in my household education was not important and working was therefore, in high school I had 3 jobs.

No one told me until I attended Benedict College that when I walked through the door I automatically had a 100. If someone would have told me that the only thing I had to do was to keep it, I would have been an honor roll students years before college. Teachers made being a honor student difficult. What also contributed to the poor grades was my interest outside of school- all I thought about was work.

See one of the things I didn't tell you was that my father told me at 15 years old not to put his name on anything or to ask him for anything because if I wanted it I had to work for it. I will say that he gave me my first car at 15 years old. However with the gift, I was told that it was my responsibility to put it on the road with insurance, gas and keep it repaired. Parents should be careful of the tough love paradigm as it can bite you if you push your children too far. A good example of this is found in a great book of **Ephesians 6:4** within the Bible.

Moving to the topic at hand, parenting business-minded children, many businesses fail not because of serious issues but because the manager can't communicate in a language his workers can or willing to understand. While running a business it is important for children to know that they need to care for their employees and their customers. In fact, the reason why many Jewish businesses are successful is because they pray for the success of their customers and employees (Diener, 2007). Having empathy helps business- minded individuals handle emotions, resolve conflicts and develop emotional intelligence.

BUSINESS-MINDED CHILDREN NEED ENCOURAGEMENT

Many business-minded children are encouraged to act like a business person at an early stage of life. This include but not limited to; personally, observing an business professional while growing up.

Business- minded child have to be taught how to count small and large amounts of money, collect money while thanking their customer, saving money, invoicing clients and record things on their own. In other words, these children must have a journal.

Mowing lawns or selling candy encourages business minded children to learn how to set up a business. Selling cookies is Girl Scout Business-minded Training 101. Yes, I was a Girl Scout who had highest in sales one year. Tell business- minded children the reasons never look down on a disadvantage person; self-motivation through setbacks will be a cornerstone that they will need to learn from because not all disadvantage persons are uneducated nor unintelligent. You can learn something great from every person.. This is a necessity as many wealthy successful people never had a smooth landing and some have been noted as being homeless.

Parents should also challenge these types of children by inspiring them think of creative ways to make money. Praise other kids around who had creative ideas, this will invariably make your own kids develop the enthusiasm as they would need to be praised. When I was younger; I often feel challenged when my parents praise and encourage other successful business-minded children and thought what about me- I am here Yet, the other children deserved the praise too.

Intelligence is a good factor, but creativity is the ruling concept when it comes to parenting business-minded children. People will always want the best, the easiest and the most attractive hence the person who offers this is the biggest bidder. Parents are tasked with the specula duty of always allowing your child think outside the box. By thinking outside the box, better outcomes and results will grace their lives.

Business-minded children willingly learn the a science of mentality, dedication, and determination. In fact, parents should encourage business-minded children to work smarter instead of harder once they master certain task.

Legacy OF LEADERSHIP

Business owners who wish to pass on family business one day or want their kids to create their own do are what should be expected of any successful parents invest into their children early. Royal families and some celebrities are taught to trained, to lead, to inspect, to oversee and to access. Children decorum, principles and leadership traits are trained and developed.

Business-minded children need to trained to become leaders, develop confidence, be assertive and decisive. The pieces of training and teachings should start like that of the royal families, pass on the family values, the family principles and the confidence needed for the task of running a business one day. Whether in the family business and another type of business setting, these steps will determine the continuity of the family legacy and the success of the future generation.

If the legacy is passing on is well and on time; the child will be have the necessary qualities required of a successful business tycoon. If parents are not business oriented but the child has interest in such; it is important to allow him or she be around other business owners, managers and other organizational leaders.

Business- minded kids must know THE VALUE OF MONEY

I once sat beside a successful businessman who is a founder of two businesses; he got mad at his 11 year old daughter because of her money mismanagement. She spent the money without telling her dad. Though the Dad later consoled her, the message was clearly sent.

One may wonder why wealthy people spend less. The fact is they know the value of money and the spirit in which money operates. As Dr. Ike once state, "Money has ears." If you call it; it will come but if you attach negativity to it – it will flee. Boy will it flee fast. Most successful business owners also know to not get sentimental in their business.

Children never think things are hard, from eating anything they want, spending on things that they find amazing; all these factors devalue the essence of money. Extravagance is a killer of funds. This millionaire was trying to tell the little kid about the need to prioritize one's needs and manage success with the utmost respect. It is good to occasional spoil your family with gifts but also tells them what need to manage.

Although I don't teach lack to my children, I do teach them to save some money back. If they earn money, it is a known expectation that they won't spend it all in one place. In fact, a lady at a donut shop influenced me not to shop there any longer. She tried to encourage my daughter to spend her entire $5. I put a quick stop to that. I do believe in being generous however; this child did not need any more sugar besides we just walked 2 miles and the day was still young and she needed to assess her needs for the remainder of the day.

When setbacks occur, those who mismanaged their previous gains will often go broke and this leads to massive borrowing thus credit card usage or unnecessary high interest loans. With high interest loans comes magnanimous interests that badly influence significantly damage the psychological pride required of any successful business person. It is wise to expect the best and plan for the worst. These teachings are what differs success from failure.

Even when the foundation seems a lot stronger than usual, there will always come a time when everything seems to be crumbling. At this point, the success and failure of a business minded person are put to test. Remember lack of preparation will always be a whirly tornado.

Separate Business From Personal Life

I once went for an eye checkup. The owner of this big health clinic came in for an eye screening. After his doctor visit was over, he draws out his debit card and paid for the eye care services. I was surprised and requested the worker to explain if this man has sold the clinic to another. The worker couldn't give any clear explanation of why he paid. When the father stepped in a few hours later and had his blood pressure checked, he also paid. At this point, I politely asked him why he is paying for the check-up since his son was the sole owner of this practice.

He smiled and told gave me this colossal phrase "business is different from personal life." He further explained that all funds are accounted for by the workers, hence it is inappropriate to cause deficits due to family or personal relationships. This is a lesson that has helped me all along, I continued to regurgitate on these words over and over again.

Most people use their business set up as a charity organization. This causes a lot of deficits, the profits may not be accurately accounted and with an increase in the sphere of influence and connections the business may experience a lot of problems due to lack of transparency.

Always teach your child the difference between business, charity, personal life and others. Another famous preacher that I had the privilege of being personally influenced by is the late Pastor Dr. Monroe. He often stated to never trust a business owner who won't buy their own product and services. Before I sell any product or service to my clients, I am the first partaker. I have to make sure that I can warranty it and stand by it. This method of listening to Dr.

Monroe for many years has made business soar. In fact, Dr. Monroe also states that "attitude is a product of belief." Therefore if your child believes that it can work and is very determined it **WILL** work.

Don't use your business for compensatory favors. This can ruin your dreams over a period of time; you can dip a hand into your pocket and do favors but never from the companies' direct collection. This lesson was learned firsthand into a three year business venture that I stopped. Parents must teach their children, "If you want someone to invest into their business they must FIRST invest into their business."

Never compromise on principles guiding any setup, this is a factor that determines how workers, family, and peers handle or interfere with your business. It is also important to know when to halt unnecessary familiarity or informality. The owner of that medical clinic may have given the money to his dad but the message I got here was that the money managerial skills of this owner are impeccable. He successful separated his personal life from his establishment's life.

This is a principle successful business-minded individuals employ in their daily lives. In fact, my dad once told me a story about a well-known man in the area who owned a chain of stores. He told me that the owner told him when he hired him as a young man to never to give any of his family any discounts regardless of who they were. Well years later the owner wife came in wanting a discount and my dad refused because upon being hired he was already warned not to do it. So the owner questioned him about not giving his wife a discount. My dad repeated his words back to him and he received a raise for being obedient. The Bible states that that obedience is better than sacrifice. Another principal that must be taught when parenting business-minded children is: "Time for business is time for business and time for fun is time for fun. With so much love and familiarity, one may mix a lot of things and lose at the end."

CURIOSITY Is THE MOTHER OF ALL INVENTION

Children are always curious, from trying to know why there is a wire in telephone, to trying to figure out how to open and reset the cellphone. At this stage, it is almost impossible to satisfy their curiosity. Exploit this developmental stage of life. Being curious about how the world works is a precursor to creating how to aid it or add to it. Business-minded children will grow up to be lifelong learners, as they will always look for ways to improve themselves, their business or the business that they manage through quality customer service, product and service innovation.

To inspire your children who are business savvy, always encourage them to start new hobbies, pursue new interest and goals no matter how esoteric it might be. Try to take them around other businesses showing them how things are and be ready to expect the questions of why and how. This will allow them to use their 21st Century Skill of comparing and contrasting. It will also remove the mindset of timidity as children who don't ask questions or want to know little or nothing. It is always wise to ask a question especially when one is not clear on something. Parents should ask them questions on why their toy talks, what makes their toy talk and what causes theirs shoe make noises. Perhaps due to a sticky floor or maybe some trinket on their laces. With these questions, they will try to know why this happens, their curiosity will help them to develop knowledge and the will always find ways to improve their personal life and business life.

Most innovations and inventions all started out of a mere curiosity. Asking the questions of why and what if; helps to business savvy individuals handle the problem of how. Through developing an hypotheses the explanation or reason is made very clear.

Enlist The Support Of Others

Being able to relate and support others is an invaluable skill for any leader. Successful people in business and leadership positions understand the importance of empathy, goodwill, and positive human and social connection. The first impression you give to people can determine the type of relationship you will end up having in the future. Even when you can't help the situation, always let them know you really care and be willing to assist if it is within your power and jurisdiction.

Learn to respect your children's individuality, their opinions and encourage them to open with their emotions and feelings. This helps them understand what others feel too, and can help kids develop a strong sense of empathy for current and future business partners and others. Those they helped today may be able to give them a helping hand on tomorrow. Hence it is good to treat those you see with utmost respect and empathy as my former church use to say, "the same people that you meet on your way up are the same people that you will meet on your way down.

GIVING BACK

Giving back might contradict the propositions where I started the importance of separating personal life from business. These two skills are actually different and noble. Business-minded individuals understand the importance of cooperate and community social responsibility. A good business-minded individual will make the world a better place not just for themselves but for everyone. Giving back is one of the ways to accomplish this goal.

Encourage your kids to give back, helping the neighborhood, doing things for their community, friends, family and for elderly. Children should be taught to give. In fact, children should be taught that in order to get something you first must make room for it by giving into that thing that they wish to have.

Moreover, business-minded children should also be taught that when they give something of value, it may not be given back in the same manner or by the same person that it may have given too. Teach children the savviness of good business by helping those they may not have a personal relationship with. In fact, if you ever want to give, please consider giving to the Single Parent Institute 501 © 3 nonprofit by contacting singleparentinstitute@gmail.com or to the Miracles N Learning Scholarship Endowment at Benedict College. No monetary donation is too small or too large. The Single Parent Institute will help single parent families and the Miracles N Learning Scholarship at Benedict College will students obtain money for books when the fund reaches $10,000, it will be distributed to help college students attending Benedict College regardless of their GPA; if they do the necessary requirements.

With teaching business minded children the art of giving, you are paving the way for your child to learn the skill of giving back this will also help them foster a sense of community from within the location of their businesses. This is a quality that will attract more people to him or her and their businesses. It is unattractive to be overly stingy, stingy people lose allies and allies are the bedrock of successful businesses.

Most billionaires and millionaires are popular because of their charitable giving and giving back attitude. This qualifies you as a good citizen, generous achiever, and attractive citizen. A good name are intertwined with your business, any character assassination via bad comments or behavior can lead to negative effects. This will be exclusively explained below as it takes years to build a good reputation and five minutes to destroy it.

Learn which battles to Ignore and which to fight

Earlier, I stated that; "Many people would agree when parenting the business-minded child, there are a lot of don'ts that you must allow the child to do. For instance, every child is taught to never talk to strangers however those who are business-minded know that communication and networking are essential when building a brand." Children are trained to report any provocation to teachers, parents, and elders.

To be a successful business leader, you need to be the General of your own army; a true general never retreat and never surrenders. When business-minded children faces challenges from peers and playmates, it is easy to run and report it but training them to stand and defend themselves in a way that is both respectful yet leaves no misgivings.

Hence, when your child runs to you reporting that Junior said my head is big, sent him back and tell him to defend himself against junior instead of telling him to go away and play with another playmate. With this, the child will not run from challenges and invariably will come out stronger and more equipped.

During my days being bullied in elementary school, it helped to shape my business-minded ways. I had to find a hustle and find a way to get out of things that I had no interest which led to me becoming a business person as a child. In fact, my youngest memory was when I was on the school newspaper and I was writing an article on safe sex and STD's.

Even at a young age, I like using illustrations and props. To make the article more practical, I went to the health department requested some free condoms so that I could sell them for $1 to all the kids who were picking on me. There were 12 in a brown bag. After the pilot was proven successful, I earned a lot of money because back then kids wanted to prove they were doing grown things even if they were not. That was my candy money because at the time my dad only gave me $1/ month and I needed money to get what I wanted more quickly. Even back then it was hard to survive off of $12 a year.

In the present world, many things will bully us, environmental factors, economic factors, background and even natural disasters but to be successful we need to stand out and raise our heads high. Teach your children to never back-off from their fight, in the business-minded world only the strong will learn to persevere and survive harsh and challenging conditions. This ability to survive is what defines your success in daily dealings as parenting business-minded children.

A popular Korean politician "Sambong" faced many challenges in life, he came up with a motto which guided him all through his life. This is "either I live mercilessly or I die mercilessly" He eventually became the first prime minister of Joseon Kingdom (Korea) after passing through difficult conditions and persecutions. It will be to your best advantage and their best interest to always expose your kids to the harsh and competitive reality of the world instead of making them feel as if the world is a bed of roses. The world is not a bed of roses and can never be.

In fact, the struggle starts from fertilization of an ovum when millions of spermatozoa are given the arduous task of fertilizing one egg under harsh and difficult conditions. The others who fell at this task are washed off as menses while the victorious one is celebrated as a pregnancy. Teach them that through arduous fighting, a great victory will surface.

Be A Risk Taker

I may have started this piece by giving insights on my experiences as a child born in an business-minded home. Let's define what business-minded means. A person with the ability to organize and operates a business venture and assumes much of the associated risk. The venture must be risky financially, psychologically or otherwise. Being a risk taker is what differentiates a manager from other levels of serving an employee.

From the early stages of life, we are trained to depend on parents for food, clothing, and security. When parenting business-minded children, it is your duty to give children another viewpoint, tell them they can also take the risk of acquiring certain things to themselves that might demand time.

As he or she grows, being exposed to ups and downs of life gives children the required strength to face the bigger world. Once they develop the spirit of venturing into independent duties, your problem is half solved and your lesson well taught.

Business-minded children can't do without risk and risk demands independence. Independence after much struggle gives the way for more ventures which will subsequently end in some type of glory.

The History Of A Business Is Just As Important As Forward Thinking

If there is anything I love more than leadership that is history. In my next life, I will eventually be a historian for the family. When growing up, my great grandma Evelyn, Great Grand Aunt Mary, Great Grandaunt Muddah and Grand Uncle Levi always taught me the history of things. Children remember history more than anything you could possibly imagine. History gives a clear picture of what happened in the past, what is happening now and what may happen in future. This is important in decision making both as an administrator and an business-minded individual as it gives forecasting abilities for an excel spreadsheet.

Inadvertently, history paves way for better understanding of the future and the reason why things are way they are today. Many parents shy away from this responsibility or simply regard it as irrelevant. Stories inspire the children, it influences their mindset and helps crave some business savvy factors.

For a business venture, there is a need to get facts about what happened in the past, why it failed, why it was successful and why it never happened. Always remember to pass down vital information to your children. With this they will learn to make amends, solve old issues and plan for a better outcome. I am a strong advocate to understanding the future by learning from the past. People of different age groups, it is important to know your footing, your past, your history and the need to make amends or continue the trend.

Government, organizations, leaders, and scientists all employ the knowledge of history in their daily dealings. Without the past, the present can't be and without the present the future is void.

Also, teaching and telling stories of past to your kids build a very strong bond as the feel connected, important and valued. You can only tell your story to the people you value; hence the children will have this inbuilt sense of belonging. The bond between successful people is only expressed through history, with this knowledge; your kid will also keep their own history and it will be a memory to be passed down.

Encourage The 21st Century Skills

The twenty-first-century skills emphasize on soft skills and character traits. This is basically creative thinking and curiosity. Over the years there has been a surge of changes, the 21st century has witnessed the greatest surge due to enabling environment and focus created by schools of thought and inquiry.

Recognize your child's cognitive skills, soft skills and put them in the right educational and enabling environment. You may wish for a Medical doctor but the cognitive skills point towards a medical technician, this will give you the idea that is the way to go. In fact, you can still have a Doctor in your family who may also work in tech. I am living proof of it as there are various types of doctors. Care based centers and institutions now employ the mechanism of identifying strengths and giftings of an individual because children do great in their perspective field of interest. The business-minded kid should be allowed to explore the their gift of what nature has given him. Parents should encourage knowing more about technology outside of the computer as this help cognitive development early in life. By all means, the educator in me who love technology yet I am highly encouraging you to let you child write using pen and pencil. The more you don't use a skill, the easiest for it to disappear.

Never restrict your children to the old way of doing things, learn to go with the trend as this will make things easier in the future. The typical exposure to these skills will help business- minded children overcome challenges. Sometimes it is just best to also always a child to be a child. Allowing them to watch their favorite TV shows or to explore their personal space but always look out for their area of interest so you can channel them towards their path as early as possible.

There Is GOLD In Two Way Communication

Inspire your kids to negotiate conflicts without becoming disagreeable. This helps model how they will collaborate with others, how they express their feelings and boost their communication skills. It is not enough having all the qualities when you can't express yourself in a marketable manner. If your communication skills are poor; ideas and concepts may evaporate even before getting started.

Furthermore, it takes a bit more to convince others to believe in what you believe. Business-minded children typically convince others that their product or service is worth its weight in gold; every time they want to venture into anything, good communication skills come top in anything that involves the second or third party.

Maintain Good Level Of Personal Security

Plagiarism is a crime, many scientists and great men have been accused of plagiarism, but the end results always very vague. It is always safer to protect your ideas, beliefs and methods through licensing, service or trademarks.

Success in business is possible when you know what others don't know yet; the secret of a very successful venture depends on how you protect and project your ideas. Although introversion is discouraged, it can also be a force of reckoning in this aspect. Extroverts tend to reveal a lot and achieve a little. It is important that parents of business-minded children teach their children or foster children the importance of keeping certain ideas and things to themselves. This will prepare them for greater challenges in the future. This is essential, it is important to maintain a certain level of security especially when it is strangers that the child must communicate with in order to get a sale. It may be safer to have a sales team so that it will limit stranger interaction if you feel uncomfortable with someone.

Telling the child to close the door when strangers leave; talk quietly while the discussion is going on can go a long way in providing them the necessary level of personal security and etiquette needed when discussing business matters. Nelson Mandela learned at an early age to be the last to speak. In America, the opposite is taught. However whenever you are looking at great people, they are always the last to speak.

Certain things are meant for the mind and not to be exposed, success is to be celebrated but not all success is meant to be exposed. These little things will help in molding their lives as they will never lose guide against total strangers and spies. For instance on social media, there are people who lurk and will never comment so if you don't have the right tools to check who was looking at your page, you may potentially put your ideas on blast intentionally to those who may not mean the children and business any good.

During business ventures and start-ups, ideas which could have been protected may be leaked to rivals. This mistake may be too late to correct in the ever competitive world. Generally, it is important to teach your kids to listen more and speak less, listening puts in more knowledge, speak leaks more knowledge and less is acquired. For instance most humans are born with 2 ears and 1 mouth therefore it is to each human advantage to utilize their ears more and their mouths less.

Some Things You Don't Play With

We live in a civilized world; the human society is governed by rules, regulations, and laws. It is imperative that even the most ambitious of all men might meet demise (damaged career) if he or she trespass the laws of the land. This also concerns people who wish to venture into business. Be clear and explain to your business-minded children the need to always respect the law and live up to principles.

Adaptability is expected when one enters a new environment, it is also important to know the basic laws governing the business sector as to be forewarned is to be forearmed. Knowing the laws, its provisions and laws is a great factor the business-minded child and their parents should never ignore.

At home set certain rules that are not meant to be broken and once your kids break any of them, it is wise to redirect them by reestablishing the rules of your home. It may advantageous to hang up rosters for house chores must be kept, the environment must be clean and other things deemed necessary must be obeyed.

Speaking of a clean environment and business, I often tell my children, I have never seen a wealthy person living in a dirty house. Money when it is call correctly likes order and organization. As a parent raising future successful businessman and businesswomen, remember to always back their business with legal standing meaning make sure you get an operating license and/ or retail license if products are going to be sold. In the words of the Bible- "Give unto Caesar what belongs to Caesar."

No Need for the IRON FIST

It is important for parents to sometimes be assertive. Getting an understanding of your kids needs are important as many will be defiant. However, my father was a strict Man, from making you realize your errors to telling you the impact of their negativity. He always overdid it when issuing out the punishment. I don't even recalled being disciplined by him or getting grace from him as a child or as an adult.

Remember, not all errors need major or instant corrections; some certain things should be ignored and some need to be criticized. Habitually going hard on your children affects their confidence, their self- esteem and possibly their level of comfort including their way of thinking. Never treat your kids like those under intensive military training, allow a lot of errors, overlook certain things and let them decide to be good themselves.

Instead of always using authoritative parenting remember there is a way to get the bad and prodigal child to act better. Yes business-minded children are children with different attitudes during different times of the day. So expect that when speaking about the business, their level of sitting still may vary.

Ultimately remember that children hardly forget the impact of such treatment. One of my favorite movies to integrate into my parenting classes is Men of Honor. One of the highlights of the movie is when it shows ASNF on the radio then later shows its meaning: *A Son Never Forgets*. The same is true for children. Business- minded children will not forget how you treat them therefore if you want a return on an investment, you must treat your children kind and spend time with them.

For an business-mindedly minded child, all aspiration, dreams, and confidence vanish into the thin sky when confronted with over competitiveness. Over competitiveness has damaged many homes, some children even as an adult feel loved and others feel dejected and rejected. The feeling of inferiority complex makes unimaginable dreams impossible. One of the factors to consider during parenting is equal love and care. Even if you have a special one at heart, never make out obvious gestures and it is a misnomer for a parent to love one child and hate other. Treat all and every child the same way, recognize special treatment when it is necessary but never overdo it as a child never forgets how someone made them feel.

Humans generally are in constant check and balances as they give special attention to those who are loyal to them and tend to disregard those who are disloyal. However, parents should never succumb to such daunting schemes; instead they should recognize some children are born with different ideas and ways of living life. Don't expect all to be over quite, loyal and obedient. For business-minded children, this is the stepping stone towards greatness, with enough praise and love during childhood.

For the child who never received proper care and love from their parents, either due to bad they tend to be easily agitated and aggressive when derogatory or annoying gestures are used on them. Most of our adulthood behaviors are influenced by childhood traumatic experiences, the brain is a powerful computer, and those memories often spring up when similar occasions present it.

Get Rid Of The Habit Of Procrastination

Procrastination is a language that successful people abhor. Chances and opportunities are meant to be taken. When you fail to use the ideal chance, there will always be a poor result or no result at all. Most children with the business-minded spirit will also be known as risk takers.

When parenting, never allow your kids to wallow in self-regurgitation and unending fear whenever something they can do comes to them. Why? Who wants to live life full of regrets. Business-minded children should never be allowed willing miss a good opportunity.

Tell them to be bold, be confident and never be afraid of failing. From failure comes success and those who are afraid of failing never really pass. It will be important to ingrain this trait into your kids. this will help them to try out new ideas without fear or doubt. Doubt may exist but confidence keeps them going.

There are a lot of do's and don'ts when training children, to make a difference sometimes it is important to do things the other way round. Inventions all started from doing the *don'ts* and innovations sprung from changing the way of doing the *do*.

Even when business-minded children get rejected; it can be a force to beckon with later on in life. Never limit your kids' too few ideas as you might be limiting their greatness. Assuming what would have happened if the parents of Bill gates never allowed him to use the computer system or never allowed him to explore his dreams; can imagine what could have become of the technology world and him? The power of trying new things can never be underestimated and the stance of never failing to try out new things is a welcome development of inquiry that most child development centers and preschools embrace.

Be Careful How You Say It

Freedom of speech is even on almost all laws of the world. In our society today, freedom of speech is on the rise. The resultant freedom after speech can be met with unwelcoming attitude.

Many psychologists have pointed out the reason why some children never confide in their parents. Few negative experiences can be enough to ruin the trust a child needs in life. When a child speaks up on awful things, never treat it as a bizarre. Use caution and try to compromise while giving the necessary lessons. Also try to relate their ideas to what he or she has said to real life experiences but not dampen their ideas.

Don't jump to conclusion. When parenting business-minded children never abuse the open door relationship; rather know that you must establish it. Respect them and this will make them confide in you and tell you even greater secrets that you could never have imagined. Children tend to tell their mothers more secrets because women are more conservative and less aggressive than men; as the can flare up when certain things get to their knowledge.

This attitude is not encouraging, be friendly and accommodating even when you are mad at something. Never allow your facial appearance pass the wrong information to your kids. Such information is that you are so made that your love for them has diminished. In my parenting classes, I teach unconditional love.

Children look people into the eyes, the make their judgment from here. They consider whether to trust you or not from a single glance and whether they will continue to do so in the near future.

This is an inherent trait which compensates for their lack of powerful reasoning at this stage of life. Always smile when necessary and advice more than you scold. This familiarity is important for a healthy parent-child relationship.

God Should Be A Factor

Unarguably we all tend to forget things of God whenever we are not in so much need. Which is the wrong way to be. In fact, we should rejoice when Joshua 1: 8 comes into play. God promises us in Ephesians 3:20 that He will do exceedingly and abundantly more than we can ask or imagine.

In our lives, we need God's grace. As a parent never teach your children to abandon their ways of faith. As Dr. Ike often contended that the belief first starts in the mind therefore faith also starts there too. This is important both for business-minded children morals and character of their personalities.

The US currency still recognizes the supremacy of God. As you strive to make your child the best in life; never let worldly things compromise the spiritual aspect of life. Remember money is a spirit with ears. Therefore if you bless God who is also a spirit with what He has given you; it will return back many times over. Some biblical stories to examine are the Parable of talents, the 10 virgins but only 5 was wise, The 5 Lampstands and also understanding the law of sowing and reaping.

To be successful, one needs the moral, social and economic footing. Wealth gotten from ill ways should never be encouraged. Moral principles guiding business and business-minded children should be kept even when it can be detrimental to success and profit.

With this as the hallmark of parenting, you rest assured that your efforts will not be in vain. Parenting business-minded children is an arduous task, the joy and the love is what keeps us great parents going hence never lose focus on this great task.

References

Browne, Thomas, Sir, (1886). Sir Thomas Browne's Religio medici, Urn burial, Christian morals, and other essays. London: W. Scott

Curley T. (2016). 13 habits of self-made millionaires, from a man who spent 5 years studying rich people. Retrieved from https://www.independent.co.uk/life-style/habits-of-self-made-millionaires-life-advice-a7504706.html

Eikerenkoetter. F. (2008). Thinkonomics. Retrieved from www.scienceoflivingonline.com/thinkonomicsebook.pdf

Monroe. M. (Nov 13, 2017). HOW TO BECOME A LEADER Break away from your struggling mindset. [Video file]. Retrieved from URLhttps://www.youtube.com/watch?v=1FMUysy5fss

Perry, T. (March 21, 2008). *Meet the Browns* [Video file]. Retrieved from https://www.youtube.com/watch?v=1L4bBQLAFZ4

Robbins, D. (2000). Men of Honor. [Video file]. Retrieved from https://www.youtube.com/watch?v=c6JMswmgfps

ABOUT THE AUTHOR

Dr. Quaneck R. Walkes is a native of Sumter, South Carolina. Dr. Walkes is an Author, Ordained Minister, Certified Parent Instructor, Publisher and IT Professional. She graduated with honors from Argosy University, North Carolina Agricultural and Technical State University and Benedict College.

Dr. Walkes has over 13 years of experience as an experienced educator. She is an experienced parent in multiple parenting styles that include but not limited to: a biological parent, co-parent, stepparent, married parent, divorced parent, foster parent, godparent, homeschool parent, child advocate.

Dr. Walkes has experience as a poet, motivational speaker, college mentor, after-school program mentor, grant finding and writing, Information Technology college and university instructor, author, tutor for various professional disciples that include but not limited to music, social media branding, computer science, programming, marketing, technical and business writing, literacy and career change, K-5 paraprofessional, technology trainer, elementary PTA vice president, Graduate Teaching Assistant, corporate technical writer, technology solutions administrator and web designer.

She is available for family behavioral modification, parenting plans, family mediation, mentoring, consultations and for speaking engagements at your organization or church as it relates to families, education and technology. She can be reached via email singleparentinstitute@gmail.com.

Dr. Quaneck R Walkes

www.ingramcontent.com/pod-product-compliance
Lightning Source LLC
Chambersburg PA
CBHW071157220526
45468CB00003B/1059